# SHEARSMAN

## 97 & 98

### WINTER 2013 / 2014

#### GUEST EDITOR
#### KELVIN CORCORAN

*Shearsman* magazine is published in the United Kingdom by
Shearsman Books Ltd
50 Westons Hill Drive, Emersons Green, BRISTOL BS16 7DF

Managing Editor: Tony Frazer
Guest Editor, issue 97/98: Kelvin Corcoran

*Registered office*: 30-31 St James Place, Mangotsfield, Bristol BS16 9JB
*(this address not for correspondence)*

www. shearsman.com

ISBN 978-1-84861-303-4
ISSN 0260-8049

### Subscriptions and single copies

Current subscriptions—covering two double-issues, each around 108 pages, cost
£14 in the UK, £17 for the rest of Europe (including the Republic of Ireland), and
£19 for the rest of the world. Longer subscriptions may be had for a pro-rata higher
payment, which insulates purchasers from further price-rises during the
term of the subscription. North American customers will find that buying single
copies from online retailers in the USA will be cheaper than subscribing. £19
equates to about $29 at the time we went to press. The reason for this is that
overseas postage rates in the UK have been rising rapidly.

Back issues from n° 63 onwards (uniform with this issue)—cost £8.50/$13.50
through retail outlets. Single copies can be ordered for £8.50, post-free, direct from
the press, through the Shearsman online store, or from bookstores in the UK and
the USA. Earlier issues, from 1 to 62, may be had for £3 each, direct from the press,
where they are still available, but contact us for prices for a full, or partial, run.

### Submissions

*Shearsman* operates a submissions-window system, whereby submissions are only
accepted during the months of March and September, when selections are
made for the October and April issues, respectively. Submissions may be sent
by mail or email, but email attachments—other than PDFs—are not accepted.
We aim to respond within 2–3 months of the window's closure.

# CONTENTS

## *Death makes dead metaphor revive*

Death makes dead metaphor revive
Turn stiffly bright and strong.
Time that is felt as 'stopped' will freeze
Its to-fro, fro-to song

I parrot under feldspar slabs
Sunk into chambered ice.
Language, the spirit of the dead,
May mouth each utterance twice.

Spirit as echo clowns around
In punning repartee
Since each word overhears itself
Laid bare, clairaudiently.

Over its pools of greeny melt
The rearing ice will tilt.
To make *rhyme* chime again with *time*
I sound a curious lilt.

# JOHN JAMES

## Affection

*one does not work out of a reaction against but rather out of affection for*
*something*          —Barry Flanagan

1

guide my soul to the light from this unwholesome pit
where all is sold for an arm & a leg the stirrup pump
to no avail against the incendiary hail as countless children
hunger for tallow calling from faraway cities while radios
drone on masking the salacious trembling hand to fist
a sardine can almost fast food who wants it now
got no other option the drudgery of minimum wage
or listed in the Sunday supplement bought in the family visit
to the super store with mum & dad & baby buggy large as life
what do they want they do not know until they find the box
American breakfast with green top milk & loads of sugar
shake so nose to the ground the lengthy strap that pulls the dog
so careless like its human chancers show every piercing
& tattoo as yomping down the aisle they go no bended knee
or supplicant incense bow aroma of aftershave will do no
blessing now required as nothing told but enter pin code now
the 4x4 awaits as shriven by the carwash men as cheap as that
a quickie without the smokeless public bar the little town
not quite a capital spot to try for pollination
a double bed can wait

2

                    Fruiting bodies vintage
garment by the carpet pile grandpa full of what he's led to believe
some stinking rubbish from the daily junk adorning flaccid
regular the mat falling on us all as the queen lacks semen
popping drones following the soak of neonicotinoid

what good are they well there's munitions
pull up his joggers crossing the road against the red
two fingers to the horn the camera can only lie in shaky grey
by what stretch can this be called an art house cinema
our visions of grown up fillum lacking schedule
would you credit it best to buy your olive oil from Aldi
at least in winter bare flesh concealed from blatant view
dot & carry at the ankle loss of pace in sorry state
wrapt in a shiny body warmer Soviet black felt scarf & woolly bonnet
seeking something good to eat to take home to your kitchen
forlorn sell out of the local to the multiple estate

3

                    Bite off the
top of the morning on the high road to the bank no froth
or gain to see the pitiful junky lost to the world beside the path
would you believe it yes it is there tension of neck muscle
can't wait to get back home make fast the door rewind
the dread & disarray of the street to climb the stair
to application love of the creatures seen from the window
at the secrétaire you will continue till you ache the line
will turn & turn again in ascending barometric pressure
before you rest to reconsider what is done a draft
a pattern showing how it's made

4

                    Call-sign freedom
of the kitchen taking the bird in hand & spatchcock for the grill
a little pile of carrot slices layered in the pot for Vichy
mortared pepper bursting aroma of the juniper under your nose
man on a roll a glutton for more throw in a soupçon of garlic
pursued as Norah showed you by the glowing range so long ago
toiling in the back of the house away from traffic noise at the front
she's standing on the stair again calling your name faithful as ever

in spite of everything hot on the hob a quick sip of red
a drop to ease the perspiration dripping from your brow
another splash of southern red brought in from Carignan
Napoleonic Guards are marching on back Rod Steiger at their head
a marvellous recreation but the deadly Prussian cavalry in black
infest the possibility stifle the scenario of the struggle
all was lost but now we have to stay alive to get things done
to wish for calm & certitude resist the pelting rain
that drives us to the lee of the house flicker of
painful surrender denied

5

                    land of the free
TV direction what cost dominant intrusion severed our conversation
broken linkage in the aftermath of 1953 soon to be washing whiter
without blue or so she thought American all over as the hotter prospect
spinning like a running dog & working for the Yankee dollar
removal of hedgerow not recorded in the broken archive
never had it so Macmillan said but why should we always tag along
          behind
as in a chaingang with mist shrouding the forgotten garden shelter
corrugated pile encased in turf like a charcoal burner bonfire
arms slung over the swaying washing line you play in your bonnet
sheets of glass breaking your volunteer fall in the blink of an eye
take off your socks to feel the pain of shard extraction from your leg
feathered deep in gore a flowing dream of torture worse to come
in Castlereagh heart beating for the ravening constable any old tale
          will do
then back to your cell would you believe it take it or leave it in your
          own time
one finger one thumb keep talking swear by Almighty God the whole
          shebang
still breathing with a bloody mark on anglo conscience
no further questions asked each man & woman spoken for as beast

7

6

        In the curving
surface of the screen the news today a baleful pornographic dance
defies your sofa plump up the cushions skip the ads
the Devil now assails your weary visage
but you say Hail Mary to send him away that's what we do
say no to all his works & pomps deny send back his penetrating gaze
flick the switch tear up the card & cross your legs before the fire
of celebrity eating their way through muck before your faltering hearth
listen to what I say or speak your own sequential prayer
zap each shadowy intrusion & abide the possibility of better times
break off & rearrange your own interior without external guide
that deed of stolen thought it's beaten out of you to cut you down to size
it's take you over time in substitute Weetabix a catch phrase or two
rises in your throat you'd better believe it they want you to swallow it
proceed to eat your Horlicks in the darkened room a spark of light
in the fallen log ash before the power supply gets too expensive
cut down the cost entailed inside the home renew your Senior Railcard
drink deep from history ancient story modern pain unheimlich durance
but for a moment recall all that was not lost in the guarded outlook
of our cherished circle our careful ambience in these four walls
en garde my love a hoard of peace & happiness in time abundant
though worn out by work & visits to the doctor never cost a penny
even when strapped for cash we never lost for thought

7

        All right core rescue
a discount buy one get one free there must be a snag what choice
their sale no goods exchanged sharp elbow mob at the bolted doors
employment some privilege measured by proportional leisure
poor judgement a hazard for the unsuspecting fail to hear the tinkling keys
unwanted stock is what they queue for it's in there ready for the punters
stripped to the limit of a store card an afterthought too late
back at a northern high rise on the forgotten edge of town without a prayer

with the digital radio on now chosen over daytime telly the smelly
        dog assents
still us the object of the exercise broadband quicker than ever so watch
        yourself
though remember where you began free nuclear attack advice
that was in advance of the multiple consumer choice of piercing
debase what beauty for a *Hello* colour promo weeping wound
a surplus over youthful skin a guarantee of future anal witness
mastication before expectoration superseded by no legal aid
a cost removed by further difficult decision

8

                    Entire violation
unnatural condition of the current privation
all in it together club armchairs for some subscription fully paid
but must we succumb what can you do they say
lie down for it under the cosh & boot acceptance
a last defence of '83 now long forgotten the Peoples
March for Jobs Saint Paul what was it you wrote regarding women
Mary Magdelen of Sainte-Baume you'd never credit what has now
        become

9

*Coda: Salut*

he appears in my dream
in the glow of his thirtieth year

clad in robes of
blue & gold satin

smiling he approaches
the orchard in winter
sickle in hand

### Model City [1]

It was like reading in the newspaper one morning that the city's building minister has declared a moratorium on the construction of new hotels, and feeling yourself flooded with relief.

*

It was like only at that moment realizing how the proliferation of new hotels has filled your own head with vacancies, how each new hotel has added 50, 100, 200 emptinesses to a proliferation of emptinesses.

*

It was like suddenly thinking about the emptinesses in yourself: your body with its cells, your heart with its chambers. There were already too many emptinesses.

*

It was like feeling your cells and chambers flooded with relief, though you sense that the moratorium may have come too late, that the city with all its hotels may have already slid irrevocably into vacancy.

## Model City [2]

It was like studying plans for a concentric model city consisting of rings of houses and gardens, factories, markets, a library, a crystal palace, a "farm for epileptics," and a "home for inebriates."

*

It was like looking at a close-up of the concentric rings in which life is to be parceled out, ordered, rendered spatially lucid, and noticing, behind the circular railway, an allocation for a jam factory.

*

It was like imagining strawberry and raspberry jam circulating neutrally among the theoretical inhabitants of the model city, jam for breakfast in the gardens of the well-to-do and at the epileptic farm.

*

It was like wondering what would happen if the inebriates were to choose not to remain spatially lucid in their allotted parcel of land, if the jam were to burst out of the factory vats and cover the model city in sweet red salve.

## Model City [3]

It was like trying to find a café that was not a Starbucks or Balzac or Einstein in an unknown city known for its coffeehouses, and finally giving up and ordering a tall skinny latte with the familiar chaste mermaid on the cup.

\*

It was like resuming your walk through the unknown city holding a cup of global capital, your familiar chaste mermaid added to the thousands of familiar chaste mermaids parading through the city.

\*

It was like wondering if any writers or scientists are sitting in Starbucks or Balzac or Einstein adding to the world's storehouse of knowledge as they sip fair-trade dark-roasted liquid global capital in cups with chaste mermaids.

\*

It was like reminding yourself to add *Moby-Dick* to your Amazon shopping cart, and then passing a small bookstore with a sign in the window in the unknown language (it says: LIQUIDATION SALE: EVERYTHING MUST GO).

## Model City [4]

It was like taking a taxi out of the city to go to the beach with friends one Sunday to lie on the sand almost comatose with pleasure, to melt into the sky and feel like a sand dollar, with no possessions.

*

It was like arriving at the beach, paying the taxi driver, listening to the waves, and then noticing the profusion of shells washed up in ridged rows on the beach, the sea's depository.

*

It was like lying on the beach almost comatose with pleasure for an hour or so and then finding yourself drawn to the ridged rows of the shells, their articulated forms, their coin-like precision.

*

It was like spending the rest of the day collecting shells and only later, adding them to your possessions, remembering you had gone to the beach to melt into the sky, to lie comatose with pleasure like a sand dollar on the sand.

# Michael Haslam

## A Round Word: World

The world is too large to be held in a word,
too multifarious in meanings and too vaguely blurred
for a tune to be heard or a tale to be told.
But the word, the world is surely roundly globed
as an orb, or ringed in a circle
    as the kingcup sepal whorl of marigold.
A world is absorbed in the woods, in the words
for an earthen mould. It's the word
    not the world that is dense as the brain
in the bone-dome home of my own.
I do like to explore my mental limits. Happily
they're close at hand. Among simple words
there is a happy land for dimwits where
the world is fair. Its field is shared and varies
in exchange with deals in equity and folk and fairies.
Here for sale at stalls are idiotic coinages
as *bonnified*, a bona fide arcadia
of pastel beauty pastorally shown along with
the associated dairies. And indeed
I have myself the world personified as
all my care is for a world as mad
        as John Clare had for Marys.

The waxing year upsprung in either hemisphere,
full-breasted world! Undressed
as a cumberland wrestler, bosoms cradled,
nestled in her folded arms and partly veiled
by either flaxen or by sable raven hair,
the elbows resting on a trestle-table. This her stall
displaying all the pulchritude of ample blossom,
pots and jars for charity or profit, floral,
        verbal, choral, all for sale on gala day,
among beribboned shires and all a dale's regalia.
The band play shining buffets in the windy buff,
their brassy air-blown tunes go drifting off
among balloons and drifting sally fluff.
Fell runners puff to track and trail the crags above.
The county set in tweeds today I nearly love:
A sort of failure, falling into guff and tory
country stuff, with stirks and yowes
for sale or prizes, and a whirling well
that rises at hill foot. She gushes horizontal.
Pumps and trumpets steal the show.
The world's well-swollen tump: A Trump:
        The beautiful full frontal.

Half-way through the world, perhaps we might begin with
how to start, and you can draw your own conclusions.
You say a world is any apprehended whole, and that
the widest world is far too large for us poor moles
to dig or feel at home in, and suppose you can
rhyme that with *roaming*. This is no
creative writing lesson. You may drop your tone.
I'm saying this. I saw the horse-drawn clouds on gala day
got blown away, and it was then I felt
the well-rounded world beneath my feet
roll as a ball, and teetered off it.
There are far too many meanings of the world
to rhyme things with for profit. Half-way through
I turn to more secluded walks up sheen wood shaw.
Mill lodge. A mass of golden saxifrage. An empty stall.
The spring well hid. I come up wordless
from bank bottom to bare floor. Concrete
and scattered glass. The boarded inn.
Some scraggy grass. It seems the fair was over.
It was over there. So sometimes wordlessly
I'll walk a world of holes
and significant pitfalls. Spoil heaps. Shaly coal.

And once I would be wordless curled
inside a world-deflated ball,
        who would have much preferred
to never have been written or personified at all,
but as a worthless child in tears about the unfair world.
With mother-all he'll never now be unified
with bugger all but see her needy as a she-ghost
of the wordy world. So wordless talks: I don't see why
she need be shy before my scorn. What did her
trestle table ever bear? It only bore
some poor sepulchral ware. I got told off
for talking there, and feel ashamed for her.
A barer and more worthless stall I never saw,
and all she sold was space to let for hire,
a vesture proof against the water-spirits
of a watershedded shire. I'll say no more.
I came in at the end of the wake for the death
of the fair. No fun; no fanfare, but some
overclouded stalls, and darkened down the cinder lane,
the bluebell spinney, making for a mental,
fundamental, space of gesture: wording phrases
in a shady world, the worldly shade of sycamore.

### *from* The Modie Box

I do not understand how I can be alive while you are dead. The field white with snow and the absence of crops. Closer, the creamy brown clumps of stalks, the world after harvest.

*

They offered you to us as a possible vegetable. A butternut squash, perhaps, its pale warmth.

*

I took a box file and put everything I had of us into it—letters I wrote you, cards you sent me, photos and postcards. I stuck on a label. Its presence on the shelf reassures me.

*

Burnt toffee peanuts, orange roughy, salt water taffy, lightly sweet white wine, Constant Comment tea, raisin bread toast, salmon, Polish sausage, black olive pizza.

*

Death, resurrection, death. What could be more violent?

*

The line crackled, but I could still hear pain in your voice, if not each precise word. I fought myself not to call back, find a clear channel, extend or intensify your difficulty. If I'd known it'd be the last, I would have succumbed to my selfishness. Without such knowledge, I nearly had, anyway. I tried to allay my guilt for not calling back but wanting to by going online for flowers at once.

\*

This hunger unappeasable.

\*

There is no redemption here. Sometimes I pick up the box and shake it, and that absence, its dry sound, drags me to weeping.

\*

Hazel eyes: sunlit wheat

\*

The florist could say when the flowers had been left at the hospital, but not if—

\*

I begin to suppose I will never stop writing this poem so I, agnostic, dubious of heaven, may keep talking to you.

\*

Your body soft with loose flesh, your embrace a leaning into ease.

\*

I wrote my first poem outside of class at age 11. We were camping in Indiana, and I'd gone to the lake with my journal while you and Dad set up the Steury. As soon as I finished the first draft, I dashed back to the site to show it to you.

\*

When you laughed hard or long, you wiped the corners of your eyes.

*

After one overdose, I hallucinated. You stayed in the armchair through the night, as I spoke of the velvet softness of my growing ears, of my sister an infant again and crawling toward me, of the man hiding in the painting who—sent by you—planned to kill me.

*

My letters, largely from Los Angeles, before email, before cell phones with national calling plans. At nineteen, I signed them 'Love & revolution', as though I knew what either meant. That self-discount's too easy: I drew from experience and books. And hope.

*

A lock of hair from youth: black-brown. A lock of hair from age: hazel, glimmering honey brown, dye from a box.

*

Marigolds and mums, the only flowers she dared plant, they needed so little care.

## Salt

Flashes
on the leaves.
Your white arms
burst
beneath a pale summer dress.
Puffing and drawing the long streams
of sweet,
smokey-eyed
from your rosebud.
Red O
against a languid backdrop.
Men in brown and black trilbies
clacking their sticks
along the stones of the *Kurpark*.
You always used an umbrella
to prop up
your little hands.
White cotton down
Swans
gliding between the spray.
Only the King of England can eat them:
Not True.
No King here anyway;
not again.
Stuck now,
        sink
            later.
England is just a place.


Fog settles down over German town
Splits your insides against the verge
Screaming behind the back line

As you devour your isolation
Do you know where you've come from?
Walking down this dirty town
In a scene of cataclysm
Waiting for the upheaval of the glamour days.
I left you at the pavement
on the corner of
Wilhelmstraße;
Down by the fountain spewing sulphur in the
air;
hot, fusty springs
of
pallid, sour rain.
You never knew what was coming your way.
Curled inside a foreign tongue;
Misplaced between English soils.
All the *Kur*-waters couldn't save you now.
The red of your poppy lips
instils the opiate kiss.
Whispers
                    *Gute Nacht*


Goodnight German town.



I got your packet this morning.
Thank you for... The "Drucksache"
was most appreciated.
No time to write, I'll send this p/c
for now.
Don't forget your German script,
my dearest.
John, Jack
Jackie
        Hans.
You little devil, why don't you write?
I'll meet you at Manchester;
the 14.10 (two-thirty).
Don't forget your...

I will hope to see you then.
You don't write, you
Why?


Go
into that
vast     closed     air.
You were a long time coming,
but wasn't the wait sweet.
Now there's only mortality between us.
*Ewige Sterblichkeit.*
I won't let them take you in the dark.
Bundling
hot dense bodies
into cold metal crates.
Rising plumes of white
living air.
Trundle
click between rail joints
cart us off to the death of Brzezinka.

ARBEIT MACHT FREI

Black rails to raw stone.

The birch forest approaches.


Home
coming
the fragmented delusion
is shattered.
The glass glitters in the waste.
          Night
                    *Nacht*
Kristallnacht glass.
"You can't sit there, madam."

23

## KEINE JUDEN ERLAUBT

*Verpiss dich.*
No nonsense please, we're British.


Beside Browning's Pool
where the willows grazed
across
brown glass;
you dipped your feet
into its literary waters.
They called you to Byron's Little Venice.
*I have loved you, in the idea*
*of*
    *you.*
But reality is a different matter.
The lofty corridors of Wymering Mansions
were only a *Testament to our Youth.*
Feminism was sitting next door,
holding up
her torches of freedom,
**BENSON** *and* **HEDGES**
*for when only the best will do.*



You would be sorry if you saw it now.
Those errant bricks will not stay still,
insist on running up and down the causeway
sliding into decay
    beside
glassy-eyed neighbours.
Full smack of commercialisation.
Our old haunts grown up with
tough, wiry weeds.

No cream for the coffee
no cold meat.
Those places you warmed your glass
between your hands.
Home-coming
going
Gone.


Hate runs down walls.
We will bleed each other out.
Those former catacombs
will crawl back
to haunt you.
Linger in the skin—the teeth,
the bones.
Calcic crossbones drawing up
from the earth.
No you can't escape this one,
my love.
A prize at the core—
                    *the genes will out.*
The goal: annihilation.
War spreads to the home,
the heart.
*An eye for an eye*
Don't look back or
the wife turns to salt.
Intrinsic core.
Innate bitterness.
            You can't tame the wild things,
love.

*You cannot take the salt from the sea.*

The hour comes...

The enemy of all times plays his part
            to the end...

*die jüdische Welt Feind*
        *der ewige Jude*

Eternal,
        unending

undying

Salt.



It's been two weeks...
Haste now
my little darling
and don't forget your—
I notice your English on the last two.
I'm waiting, have been waiting
for your letter.
But I understand.
I miss you... missed you more than ever
this week.
But don't forget—
I'm...
Would you take it if you were me?
Excuse my liberty
my little darling.
I hope you are not fretting.
But you are busy, I expect.
I wish you were here
to go about with me
This week—
I missed you more than ever.



I looked for you
in those half-blurred moments
I didn't want to see.

The ghost of all this,
happened before,
rattles in cell one.
Does it matter if they take you
to the large
or small?
*kleine Festung... große Festung...*
       Close your eyes
you don't need to see this.
The quickest way to heaven is through
the *Schlauch*
the sinewy tubes pulsing with
blood and being.
We will go by the *Himmelweg*
      the path where all lives cross.

I will meet you there.

## Goatscape Monologue

When a society breaks down, time sequences shorten
by barter, insult, revenge, or neurotic symptom—
as when a man offers from his richest hand
a plastic bowl foaming with dew of daughter-
in-law, laughing, 'What law? What daughter?

    From where the partition walls have been
demolished issues a sweet smell of neglected infants
and the floury smell of pubescent boys' beds.
Foreign aliens imitate these beds for having none,
then day and night become confused, sun
comes too close to earth, and life turns
unbearable. Me, I tilled the choice garden of Grace
with its splendid trees and party of statues.
The tall neighbouring structures are collapsing
oversight. That exposed wall—
I broke into a sweat then a run when I felt it
lodge in me. It conjures disaster as a date palm
conjures dates. For beyond the city wall it's not clear
that the roaming goats are goats.
Even the smallest goat may be a disastrous blend
of man and dog. I wouldn't know how
to broadcast their number for our dear children
of the cloud. Even without coupling,
the dogs found their folk like a 'big thing',
a second head staring from behind your face,
your heart after you, beating its pulp.
They make room only for a single cause
to absorb all causality in their vision, everything
seen *as if.*
    As if; that was what I called it
when they stood around my bed, took my pulse,
crowned me with parsley to make sweet sport

of fears. Fear that if you fall asleep
some number will grow in your brain until
there is no space for you inside it fear that you lie
on a glass shelf of fear that you'll knock your bowl
from absent-mindedness or loneliness onto the glass
and break into screams and so fearful betray yourself
and speak those fears...
     Their mixture of cruelty and credulity
has assumed the proportion of myth.
Under the feet of their leader the earth never grows
again; he need only be himself
to establish his enmity's third remove.
These days I see the very real power the right costume
can exert. I grow more and more daring:
pleated Persian trousers, sweeping cloaks, wraps, shawls,
veils, diadems with stupid expressionless stones,
even a carnival mask that reminds me of a dog we had
who behaved as though he wore one.
     Camouflage is an unstable memory that pools
into the deadpan. Since envy and solidarity are better
than pity, I have offered up fireless offerings to our
cumulus children again. And they have come back to me,
as heavy a burden as ever, and so our bonds of revenge
mature, and I see they have borne us
no reason at all to wonder.

## St George's Fields

*Two of the author's relatives are buried on Leeds University campus. Leeds General Cemetery, which had become overgrown, was taken over by the university, and most of the gravestones were demolished to make way for a park in 1968.*

In the soaked towns where the Pennines hunch,
terraces cling to absent glaciers:
Wellington's memorial pokes the thaw
but not forgetfulness, as a snow-line

packs against Slaithwaite, and a dry-stone wall.
Mill ponds poach foam and defreeze in Batley
before the pull to the family bones
by the bleached library that stakes the hill.

WILLIAM ROWLAND peered over the soot
and gloom of Georgian stone, now enclosed
by Geography and its erasures,
my umbrella that spiders in the gale.

SAMUEL ROWLAND is flat round the chapel
like an afterthought: lucky at least
to ward even a daubed plot in Holbeck.
The gravestones pull away from the nave,

as my trainers smudge mud from windscreen names
after name. I pocket embarrassment
by a lodge and astronomical digs;
picture crushed stones returned to their quarry.

These gravestones were desecrated like teeth
extracted from the skulls below, quiet
as this rook that stands in for sorrow,
pitched in the crumble of marble saints.

Did diggers cut the cut names back to sand
and university hands tame bunches,
then rubbish the pin-cushion flower pots?
Only an advert in The Yorkshire Post

saved others. Even with a brother
in nearby Ganton Mount and a poet
burrowing Mercia and the blue wounds,
you were surplus, and required space.

The university is aggressive,
acquires majority shares and holds
stones at tibia length for contractors,
then designates the field's chapel as

special, of historical interest, more
architectural than working-class bones.
After, Somerset House loses the tombs,
and fire ticks the Bursar's photographs.

The remaining graves cluster the alders.
Visitors now pay homage to a sod:
death chunked the university's Raum
so it bulldozed the shade and lingerers.

The rich are stubborn in their sunken tombs:
GEORGE NUSSEY, late dyer of Bishopgate,
departed this life but not his text;
a circular angel whipped to a ghost.

Please Respect the Act of Parliament
for Quiet enjoyment and rest. Games
cannot be Permitted. Dogs must be lead
in the interest of Public Health and grass.

Cooperation of the dead would be
appreciated. Last year's leaves
log the spot, empty as their branch;
its path leads only to a public bin,

neoclassical grave turrets, twisted
and locked in an ever-expanding beech.
The sun is coined in fibula trees;
shines on petting, heavy with a lunchbox.

Soon hail pelts my sagging plastic and drips
as I crab past the haphazard years
of names: Washington followed by the thrush.
The weather of austerity: bitter

as the hand that takes and promises
we're all in it together; together
as this beneficent angel propped
on this bought grave saved from the yellow maw.

Mauve tops birth my wide occupation,
clamming mud from yet another year,
years before education could be bought
for a small mortgage, or a song for the rich.

A riveting Rowland line bucked by print
until the threat of the triple-dip;
the purge of Cameron's curtain scroungers;
the wealth of dagger cuts and generous tax;

the rupture of class and Daniel Jones
astounded at the Bullingdon Club.
We now know our place as William did,
a dream cobbler among the plough and bear,

who couldn't even nail death with a stone,
who attended siling winters on roofs
of Leeds Grammar School, excused for nights
alone with the constellations of night

so long that his fingers, spidery hand,
froze into a clutch for his indentures.
Then, among the border creep, AM ROWLAND,
wiped into hiding through years of sedge.

WILLIAM ROWLAND rescued from slate
and desecration on yearly name-stones.
Somehow, among the hate, hangs Osborne's smile.
Competition is good: sell the dead

for bucks, our star-crazy cobbler, quick
as lime before the Leeds outcries, sullen
as ethics. Appreciate capital
and the approaching stripes that yell, BANKER!

The borrowed light in the carriage hides mist,
and the sun still gashes Warth mill and tow path.
The navvy walls cut and hang Marsden,
and birches draw silver from Polish sap.

We will shortly be arriving at deeds.
Dewsbury roofs float triangles; odd
horses dredge humps and black fields of lake.
Batley silage pits work their churn and fume.

# Marion McCready

## Three Poems

I

The thin wrist
of my hydra-tree.
    All cartilage and bone,

exposed nerves
    to the bare wind.
    Flutter of knuckle-buds

growing
    from the black heart
    in the centre of my garden.

Daffodil embryos
    clutching at the air,
    sea grasses whipping around us.

Your stare.
    Everyone chooses,
    not everyone has chosen.

II

I watch the kindling-men
eat themselves.

The yellow candour
of the flames,

the calm animal of it,
tame

through the white-hot
transparency

of this telescopic tunnel
into nine circles of hell

in my living room.
The four bodies bow,

burning.
I watch the kindling-men

eat themselves,
ashes to ashes.


III

Red tower topped
with beacon tealight.
Red cocktail,
slice of lime climbing
over the lip of the glass.
The sails of your elbows

pointing towards me.
Blue-checked sleeves
of your arms unfolding.
Our hands navigate
the pine table, meeting
below the lighthouse
of the candle, rising
above the lava
of the cocktail.


## We became as the Golan Heights

*(after Yehuda Amichai)*

we became as the Golan Heights
dipping into each other

your eyes     crab-brown
Galilee boats     wood floats

tearing through holy water

we conquered the Beatitudes
orange scrub     livid as hellfires

hypnotised by the riddle of the sea
we looked over the blue eye of the Galilee

until the snake-lights of Tiberius
choked into colour     stilled fireworks

on the shoreline and we became
as the Golan Heights

dipping into each other


## Song of the Jaffa Gate

hot sun     hot stone     sun-caught
illuminate     the city waits

enter in through my arch
through my sleek bend you turn

mother     father     daughter     son
I am the herald of Jerusalem

mother of stone     birdsong wall
folded prayer-tears endlessly fall

they sell bread at my feet
taxi through my elbow

I meet myself within the Jaffa Gate
where I wait for you     my friend

## George Messo

### Autumn Lars

A thought grows deep inside the apricot.
A thousand miles from here
hoar frost dusting an arctic scythe.


### Poems Lars

Going, there is a letter.
Clearly you can read between the lines.
An open door, its tone is mostly wonder.

Years ago we found you laughing here
and piling stones into a poem.


### Lars in his Library of Forgetting

Essentially
his scholarship of broken bowls
and vanishing signs

shows himself his labyrinth.
But still he's there
because

some lend, his friends,
their pliant weight
against his path:

them struggle and leave,
then reappear again.

## A Lars of sights and smells

Those dry late winter mornings
when mud lies baked on roadsides

and on tyres and flicks off
leaving a broken trail where the tractor

shudders into life and moves away.
That's what I like.


## Visioning Lars

At night
alone in the forest,
a vast breathing.

You stumble
on the sudden wealth
of a ruin.


## Welcome

Coming home
sunlight's door into the dark
half-closed half-open

I see myself
clearly indistinct
against the background

of an overwhelming thought
going home,
going deeper.

## Go

Looking for a lost friend
you follow a path

deep in the throat
of a silent forest.

Late and by yourself
you come to a wide river,

on the far bank
the empty boat is tethered.

Now that you know where he is
how are you going to reach him


## Yes and No to Everything

Clouds across the lake
like a bad mood sealed
inside an envelope.

News arrived
down networks
of the inaudible.

Small filled space
becoming weather.


## A Dwelling Place for Lars

We sat
with morning in the room

until the grey walls turned blue
and the breath went out of him.

No slowing down
or sudden exhalation

of a dying wish. Just
my father, dead.

And when I drew the blind
all the breathing creatures

were gathered
and pressed to the window.

## Incognito

In Ottoman poems
I have observed

the concluding stanza
typically carries

the poet's name,
a signature of sorts

and what is more
Lars Pettersson,

whose reedy breath
plays like wind

through derelict rooms,
has often heard it said

all language is a longing
for home

## Lockers and Lars

The lake's ingenuity
for hiding things.


## Oared

The fetus knows everything
said Lars

but slips from its dark
into ignorance

         like a boat
drifting over a shoal.


## Lars & Lars

When Lars Pettersson
came to visit

he said     first
someone else is here

who
    *you've never met*
and second

*he's in me*
by which

      *I mean*
*let's find*

*the other you*
*to greet him*

and the four
of us sat

at this very table
Lars there and me

fingering my tie
exchanging glances

**Avant Garden**

He called the stones

        wild         (they do not remember)


others called them     found
as if a boy                or Ian Hamilton Finlay
just found himself     with the stones. On the beach he stumbled
                upon stones.    Hunted among &
             he picked
                stones at his hand. He
placed them in a garden.
        The furthest point in
Scotland from any sea.         After his death the garden
        was
           preserved.         The stones are
beautiful             taken & tame.

## Final Sonnet?

How strange to be gone in a minute!     like
a sonnet. dear Berrigan
hello. He died before     it is time
to turn
to drown steal his book. Hello. What time is it in
is it always 5.15 am with you     or
does time disturb you or
me? It is 2.03 am on the 30th of January, a
Wednesday. He died dear Hollo.
Love, why do you always take my heart away?
They say I love you & the sonnet
dead is not is dissolution.     If
I sometimes                    seam    , nevertheless

my heart still loves, will break.


## (Un)Donne Sonnet

My God!
Take me


## The Sonnet Drive

If I sometimes forget
to break to turn
it is because I am carried away. I am no one
to drive the car the Sonnet Machine. I turn to sonnets.

The Sonnets are the pure products of
the Sonnet Machine. To break it new!
The hungry dead doctor breaks into The Sonnets.
The Sonnets turn him in. To seam!

He does not love sonnets. A crab
in a box. America in a sonnet. He drowns
the sonnets but The Sonnets are not dead. They are
hungry. They eat the crab. They cut its legs off.

The crab is not
crab. The legs go crazy. They crab.

There are no dead in the Sonnet Machine. They took its brakes away.


**[I forbid you maidens all / that wear gold in your hair
to come or go by Carterhaugh / for young Tam Lin is there]**

I so fair
    & full
        of flesh
           am feared
it be my self    am phibian
           am newt / snake
             a hand to hold frog flesh
Janet    li
on limbed (what I) me in your arms your hair your mantle your kirtle
above the knee your maiden head
           the bridle ring
& you will
        father flesh
        bear the
        blame the
        love
your son out of
sight.

had I known Tam Lin
this night. naked knight.

# JOHN WELCH

## At Ranters Lodge

He took his bath with unalloyed satisfaction between four bare walls, whereon certain dimly-curtained squares in the extended whiteness indicated the exile of all art except that of the air, the sun and the wind... 'I mean that it's like the way you feel about things' she explained, 'when you hear the rain outside, while reading a book. You know what I mean. Oh I can't put it into words...' I know just what you mean' he said.

—John Cowper Powys, *Wolf Solent*

June 9th 1746
At Southwell the farthest village
Some very old men attended
My mouth and their hearts were opened
The rocks were broken in pieces
And melted into tears on every side
Charles Wesley, *Journals*

Fortuneswell... The only place on Portland with a pretty name but the town itself is of a plangent self-assertive devil-may-care ugliness. Some giant, when it was building, must have thrown a few handfuls of dry cement on it, and nobody since has swept them up... a pretty cottage in Portland would be like lipstick on a fishwife.

—Aubrey de Selincourt, in the series 'Visions of England'

*Ranters Lodge on the Isle of Portland in Dorset was formerly a Methodist chapel, and opposite stands a building formerly used as a mortuary and known as The Dead House. Conjuror's Lodge, nearby, was another Methodist chapel set up in the early nineteenth century by a breakaway group who refused to renounce a belief in witchcraft. Southwell is a village on Portland. The Isle of Portland of course has two prisons, and various other former military installations.*

No, it's not Conjuror's Lodge
And I'm not a Primitive Methodist
But here at the start of an almost-island
Opposite The Dead House
And knowing the waves aren't traffic
We'll sleep better.

It's an odd sort of house, where we sleep
On a platform right at the top.
Taking myself to bed,
There's something perfect inside me
I cannot ever quite reach—
If it could only settle on a title.
Lying here again on what she calls the day bed,
Reading steadily, sheltered from the rain
It is a satisfying room—
But the 'exile of all art'
Known by the prints
Their frames have left behind?

Well, going out walking was a way of finding
As if the words might shine back into you.
I imagined it might come together
Casually, like flowers propped in a vase
But, ornamental dust, these evocations
Stay sealed in an airtight jar

While the house fills up, with stones the guests have chosen.

...

The sea's
          just there
It's Weymouth in the mist.

The resort dwindles.
Is this a listening post?

Turn back. Thirty six pedalos
Are drawn up in ranks
And every one has its own name.

Steady rain     the verbal fuss.


## Inland

We had come, to the good place
A coastline rich with fossils.
The animals' dried dung
Being blown across the hillside
Our talk was eating the air
Like two men in a dream
And somewhere over to the left
The unreachable sea. Thrift, speedwell, eyebright
Yes, flowers with names like that.
The sea that day was breathing-still.
'Can't you see it's about trying to win something back'

…


The countryside was anxious notices.
No one's to be seen at work in the fields.

As we tread our way into it
With an awkward reverence

It's like a bad 'original print'
Expensively framed—

Crossing a fast-flowing stream,
Its unimpeachable water,

A hillside of slow cattle
Devoutly feeding

A field of long grass
Silvered in the wind, a sheet fast-flowing,

And, somewhere over there,
A fake giant with an enormous erection.

. . .

## Chesil Bank

*Die Sprache spricht and vouloir dire*—
Everywhere it speaks it wants to say,
Those times I stayed up half the night
Trying to find its singing in my head
Like tinnitus

But Babbington's Leek
Like a shy but irrepressible stranger
Is moving on to the shingle's edge.
Over the other side is all that water.
We're staying on the landward side

Where tamarisk lies stretched out over stones.
Some plants there are can colonise this shingle—
Campion, sea-kale
As if they had just landed there.
It's hard to see how they take root

And I try to be more or less contained
In what it is I have to say,
Straining against the wind
When over there I see him now
Way out on the enormous bank of shingle.

He's on his own, appropriating distance.
Fishing, or just standing there
He's starting to mean,
Maybe because there's only one of him
Whose mind goes stretched out over all that water

As if to celebrate each helpless encounter
With still more words.
Perhaps it is the sea has too much voice.
Outdistancing his code
It has a gift for appropriating silence.


## Fortune's Well

At 8 a.m. going to buy scallops
The fisherman asked 'You want shell or meat?'
Lipstick on a fishwife, what lips wish?
But something falling was the sound I heard.
This 'island' after all,
Was one enormous quarry.
At our approach each prison makes
Its special silence all around.
And we sit in our tent of phrases
To ponder the 'vision of England'.
What you watch, it is watching you here,
Abandoned installations everywhere,
Vocabulary that shifted in a storm,
The constant wind's dispersals.
It blows a fine dust over everything,
Its way of making
Gardens among these rocks
And in each careful pause for breath,
Warm scribe, these stones
Are almost all of it.
It's far too much to carry home.


## Coda

The Visitors Book:
Temporary occupation
Endlessly supplied
Terminate these applications

# LUCY SHEERMAN

## Close up of roses in the Garden with Tilley and Violet, c. 1938

All dolled up, they call on the way elsewhere,
and while he rushes to fetch the Leica
they smooth out invisible creases then
apply powder from gold Stratton compacts.
Looking up from their tiny mirrors see
hair set in waves, just patted into place,
and natty hats. They look sharp as needles.
The stop of the shutter is almost lost
in their laughter—she is still in stitches
as the snapshot pins them both together.

They take their places as shadows lengthen,
wearing glamour like good buttons. Modern.
All their cares and woe cast off, here they go,
following the rules of gloves and handbags.
What might the night not bring? San Ferry Ann.
Left behind trailing skirts and petticoats,
high necked blouses, long hair and buttoned boots.
His barking cough and the grip of rheumatics,
the scrape for money whether he worked or not.
Girls without history looking dead ahead.

Later events spill into the picture,
memories in reverse have blurred the shot
like out of focus after images.
They give the air of knowing what's in store;
her decision to have things not children,
the disappearance of the garden,
all the friends who left and didn't come back:
some scattered across the suburbs like seeds,
some lost like letters sent to empty houses.
The weather never so fine in June again.

They are garlanded with tinted roses,
pink profusion, a reckless lovely show.
Painted lips and powdered faces, tilted
towards each other just for a moment.
Light draped across them like a pale shawl.
Still slim, before the babies, she looks down
at the skirt she made herself from oddments
and the shoes that pinch her relentlessly.
Her older sister looks into the lens
as if to say 'my roses will one day be better'.

There is a kind of fleeting harmony
in the cool smiles, frozen in the moment,
as their friend called out to 'watch the birdie'.
So that later the picture came to be
a talisman, a dream of calm and hope
that the roses might be in bloom each June.
The scent of their perfume following them
even when the lovely satin jacket
with the fancy trim was out of fashion
or threadbare, the stitches unravelling.

## Things Which Had I Stopped to Consider—Really Consider—Or If I'd Been Older—Might Have Been Clues

That time we took Violet the cat—who had six toes on each front paw—up to the Blue Ridge Parkway. You said she would like to get out of the city. We opened the car door and she ran away, right into the rhododendron up the side of the mountain. We called and called—*Violet! Violet!*—but she never came back.

The time you locked yourself in the bedroom. I screamed—*don't do it, don't do it!*—but you still didn't come out.

## Things You've Said to Me Which I Still Have Doubts About

Once when he was married with two more children, my father visited you in Texas. He implied that if you didn't have sex with him he wouldn't give me your social security money. You had sex with him.

You had polio as a child.

You are a genius.

Janis Joplin used to sit and sing on your fire escape in Austin. Before the drugs, she had a voice like Joan Baez.

You were in a car wreck at 16 and went through the windscreen. This caused your epilepsy.

When you asked your half-sister in California whether she too had been abused, she almost threw up into a salad bowl.

You heard a baby crying so you called the police and social services.

The baby's relatives threatened you.

You fell into the bathtub and hit your head.

## Things You've Said to Me Which I Now Know to Be Untrue

I am an asshole.

You speak French, German and Spanish.

You once went to a nursing home to look at it, and instead of asking you to live there, they asked you to work for them.

I am just like your mother.

You once rang a publishing house. They asked you to work for them. On account of your languages.

Everybody loves you.

Everybody hates you.

None of your friends like you anymore because you're in a wheelchair.

I think I'm so great.

Everyone's a lot nicer to you than I am.


## Things You Said Which I Know to Be True

911 broke down the door.

You were lying in the bath hollering.

You didn't know who you were, who was president, or where you were.

You guessed George Bush.

## St. Justine

along the wooden barricades,
came the wolves and the revolutionaries,
gnawing at the earth and ground
of the saints of Barcelona;
and the aroma was of Death,
the death of an era of widows and dogs,
of the velvet arms of a godless kingdom;
and they wailed the gypsies plagued
by the stars of St. Justine,
lighting up the valley of olive nights
and the windows of secret gardens.
the tiger growls in hunger
for the space between life and eternity,
and the gypsy with the stump
drinks his liquor, between her lips
of pink lilies and poisoned ivy.
"weep, weep for St. Justine",
they tell the children of the Aegean sea,
who climb the dunes in droves,
washed ashore by the shipwreck
of the nymph's womb.
and the gypsies hear the sirens
off the west coast of Spain,
and they walk to their songs,
along an ether of bronze and steel,
where life is unconscious
and the only meaning,
lies in the tombed heart of St. Justine.

## Oana

"be joyful in the souls of Gods"
as the river of red crabs,
was drunk by Oana, the gypsy girl
who fashioned the face
of the melancholic and sublime poet;
she raised her breasts and he ate
from the gypsy plate, a feast
as eloquent as his words and she
corrupted his girth in times of season
and of indomitable worth.
then the armies came to Madrid,
and Oana fled to the skies of black
olives and fleshless salmon, whose
gills were filled with her jealousy,
and her empty and vile compassion.
there was no peace in the war,
and the Generals slept in her bed,
Oana the silk of Apollo and the blood
of Orpheus, with the songs of gypsies
between her legs of desire,
and her pity without any clothes;
for she raised her legs higher and higher
and the Generals drank,
toasting Oana the darkened gypsy rose.


## Seville

"the possession, the possession!"
cried the gypsies in their caravans,
traversing the ruins of Seville, where
the waters garnish the oranges
with pale wine and copper tongues.
"where do they go now?" shout
the wild children of the crematorium,

to the orgies of self-infliction, where
the daggers are drawn and slash
the fires of female innocence,
and male iniquity; "but this is not
enough", chant the soldiers of Seville,
who point their rifles at a gypsy,
with the scar of heaven on his cheek.
and they run like dogs of Pluto,
and they run like cats of Saturn,
and the flesh is eaten by mad horses
driven by the whips of the gypsies,
who castigate the living, in a house
of vodka, rum and whiskey;
"go now, go to the sea and drown!"
the seagulls hawk at the soldiers,
who lick the dust from their boots
and march in tandem through,
the ghosts of this morbid gypsy town.

### Saltgrass Lane

1
Blank as a sheet of paper
the mud shines
as the tide ebbs.

Shines blankly
before the gulls come
and the waders, piping.

Would it be the same
if I could go back
and lie down on rough grass
watching sun-lit cloud
on a September day
passing and never-ending?


2
All the world here
that isn't water is stone.

Stone and mud,
and fleshy, salt-loving plants.

Water mirrors
waders and gulls
as the tide ebbs, draining
sky from the estuary.

Now I climb the shingle-spit,
slide back, scramble over.

Over the bank the sea meets me
with a smack of light,
colour and salt-lashed air.

Behind me the lane ending at the bridge
creeps away, silver-grey as snail shine
back the way I came.


3
For an old man
who walks with difficulty
memory is to return
without a stumble.

Feet springing on the lane,
feet hanging over the bridge
where he dangles a rind

on a string weighted with a stone.
Crabs in the murk wave their claws.
The day is tense with expectation.

Legs striding, legs at ease,
body unconscious
as a fish or a bird.


4
Tern's wing and curve
of shingle-spit,
gull and lighthouse:
white echoes white at high tide
on the water's mirror.

Days, though, are visible fractions,
so many pictures shattering.
Power unabated works unseen,
sun quickening water and plant—
thrift & sea-purslane & horned-poppy.

Sand waves drive through,
clouds of sediment settle,
tides mould, unmake, remould...

Underwater, a wreck's ribs are unpicked,
currents swirl, abrade, scour,
among detritus, in nutrient dark,
algae and larvae replenish the multitude.

A father watching his son pick up a stone
sees, momentarily,
a vision of power—
the boy hurling the beach into the sea.


5
Legs with little power
and each word a stumble,

a slippery step

plunging in cracks & creeks,
squeezing out prints
of mineral-rich, polluted ooze.

Drawing a line that runs out,
finding a foothold
on a surface scribbled over:
hieroglyph, palimpsest

     *mewl   pipe   cry*

or as ducks dabble
or dunlin follow the ebb.

Step feeling after step
each word composing,
decomposing, moving on.

6
Everything here speaks of defences—

a castle built in part from abbey stone,
the concrete shell of a pillbox,
breakwaters, shingle
built up by longshore drift.

One yellow horned-poppy,
apparently with no soil to root in,
stands up between sea and castle walls.


7
I do not expect to walk here
alive again.

Nor do I wish to come
only in memory
repeating taken steps.

Or as some living phantom
who walks without touching
and the blind reaching of touch.

This was always somewhere between,
with no beginning or end,

always a place in the making
where I was happy to be.


8
As well ask the stones
who he is, the man who wanders
in and out of time—
friend and lover,
brother, father, son.

As soon ask sand and shells
which the tide covers and uncovers,
shifting them, breaking
one seeming pattern
to leave another
which the next flood breaks.

As well question the trunk
skinned white
cast up with feathers & corks.

Or the clothes left on the beach.

Naked,
he is not the one you seek.


9
On the crown of the bank
against the sky
a man and a woman walk away

small figures at a distance
between saltmarsh and sea.

Step by step
they move away,
hand in hand.

Soon there will be nothing to see,
and what you will have seen
is nothing, not a jot
of the sea they see, nothing
of sun kindling the stones
they tread on, or kiss
of salt on eyelashes and lips.

Nothing but the distance
in which they vanish,
into the world they have made
between them, where they walk away.


10
Flounders and small green crabs
are working in the mud,
bass swimming in with the tide.

Sure-footed, I stand
on slippery stones.

Gull islands, wallowing
as the tide returns,
begin to disappear,
washed smooth and shining.

## Maria Jastrzębska

### Queen of Hearts, O Queen of Hearts

a thousand times nearer
than I imagined,
is it luck dealing me your card?

Queen of spiders and ants
dragging crumbs
and white petals before you.

Queen of bread and spilt blood,
of flesh red as watermelon, wine.

Queen of the knife
and flies which crawl
into each orifice.

He sat opposite me at this table.
The cups and plates danced
as he slapped his hand against it.

Queen of hibiscus and bougainvillea,
of every long story, each fable.

Handful of garnets.
Emporium of light.

Low octave, strobe, bassline,
beat of a drum.

O Queen of the trick and the trump.
Of the leaping spark
and circle closing—

a red dust moon
bruised by clouds.

Queen of the red mouth,
vernix and afterbirth.
Coral reef, derelict fort.

Queen of a broken promise
and starless night.

Of swollen eyes, boarded up windows,
unsaid goodbyes.

Of creased time-tables, maps,
the long journey home.

Once he'd run away, turning back
to laugh. With each year
his small fists grew stronger.

Queen of diesel oil and purring motor
red sails and flags
voices floating across water.

Of herons in flight,
owls carrying prey to their young.
Queen of the grey hour before dawn.

Refuge extraordinary,
city of dew.

Rough tongue
of comfort.

Last star,
first light.

Queen of shutters banging
a parrot squawking, chairs scraped,

the creak of awnings
and the same words every morning.

Queen of caves dripping salt,
both flood and culvert, unhealed
subterranean scar

of clogged pipes, grease, landfill.
Queen of sugar heap and anthill.

He still paces, shaking
his fists at the sky.

Acid rain, fly ash,
verdigris and red rust.

Murmur unmistakable.
Clamour of old.

Twist in the road.
Wake-up call.

Heart in the mouth, rivermouth,
heart on a sleeve.
Lion-heart.

Queen of bulrushes, barges
heaving their chains.

Queen of what starts
as small ripples

of the droplet
and squall, trees torn,
of flame and charcoal.

Queen of thundersnow.

Queen of the harbour estuary
of red sky and open sea.

Queen of Hearts, O Queen.

Lady of rare hope,
carry him in your arms

as a river nudges a fallen log
or a mother lifts her child.

In the grey hour before dawn.
take him from me.


## Grave Goods

Place him in a pit, lined
with flat stones
fold his arms, leave his legs
to fall apart naturally.
Lay his tools next to him—
a heavy belt, a sickle, his quiver
of arrows, shield, antler dice,
bone gaming pieces
on a tafla board, steel comb,
an old flick knife, his strike-a-light,
joints (neat, ready rolled) a pack of three,
mouth organ already rusty.
Cover his body with planks torn
from a boat, iron rivets still in.
No matter how weary you are,
fill the pit—oval-shaped
like a girl's eye—with sand.
Fill her eyes with tiny grains of salt.
Don't jump in the grave beside him.

### nurses in white echo

pricked by roses    counterparts to be whispered
corridors lit limpid    the night watch
mist in at half-shut windows' shaded ocean
forgetting you had ever
                        passed without
a word will rattle    solitary blinds
                bleached linen
nameless    an exchange of cool greeting
sinks to the floor
                mouth to mouth
                long distance
its candle in the woods
the keys to an empty piano
                    moth-flutter in your belly
velvet lymphing and beginning to fall
from all these fragments overhung with pictures

### the new picture

draw down again    'the golden frame is Victorian'

is it getting harder to be honest

      or is it that
the way pain    burst to the sides with earth
from an abandoned street    or teeth
            like    'forward is development'

trying too hard to move
            the rose is bigger    filling the mirror
moon-faced hangman trailing rainwater from broken guttering
a bunch of memories threatening a rematch

*I thought I understood but…*
　　　since that thing in the wall appeared
　　　and left home　　simultaneously defamiliarised
somehow it got forgotten that the missing rigging
broke hairlines around clouds
　　　　　　　　　　　already gathered up
bundled into arms too weak to hold you
　　　or is it　　me　　or her
and is this really a matter for discussion


the little red boat in the new picture
balances badly on the blue of harbour
　　　　getting smaller　　it seems
summer rain blotching our picnic table with birdsong


I'm not sure I'm arguing this very clearly
but someone needs to know
　　　　　　　　that finding a hand
is not a matter of sentiment
　　just a dust of light
　　　brushing sails as dawn falls through drawn trees


out there somewhere the moor is getting bigger
and low clouds are sailing　　yes sailing　　despite critical notices
repeating the way a story envelops and tells you
yourself in low drama
　　　　　　　　bruises opening
waves grainy and static


notes for a new project　　'arsenic in the water
poisons a whole village'
　　　　　　　　but who would want to do it
plot line receding through desperate border plants for a final birthday


and still the boat moves newly out of harbour
　　　　　　　　　　　as it has for years
going nowhere　　fixed　　questions raised　　where you want it

## Le Monde Diplomatique

It appears like the moon,
its matt white skin
imprinted with tattoos.

It lies in the pile,
lurking among locals
and dailies, as clouds
ramble across the sky.

The frozen ground
is melting away.
The Wars of Africa
warm up the graphics.
Europeans dream revolt
in the lands of Che.

Outside, the flies are making
short-haul flights from stamen
to stamen on a great wall of ivy.

## The New Village

Next door, the architects move in
to the nineteenth century, then emerge
into the trending twenty-first
and stroll the North Atlantic rim.

Snow's on the church roof, and the cobbles
are mumbling with four-wheel drives,
their constant, continental drift,
here where the silk-weaving has stopped.

We've decided to split into two,
but flat-finding's like walking on ice
as the temperatures rush to rise.
Divided the calendar up too—

you get May while I march in March.
What year was the village first mentioned,
estate agent? The price of land
contours and colours the climate chart.

New, they're saying, is the new old.
The lease agreements freeze and melt.
Where the white mulberries were felled,
the land where we live's being sold.


## From *Hellenic Post*

The ancient theatre with its latest productions:
I hope you can hear me, up there at the back,
although the cicadas are repeating their lines,
and the light crescendoes from the multiple rigs
as I open just one of the fourteen grey doors
and exit the mighty black box of backstage.
As you can see, I'm playing the dark monarch,
around whom the arcs of seating are intact.
And it's you I can see, up there on the rim
of the stone web, killing lichen with your jeans.
I lurk at the centre, silent and distant,
till I sense your shifting, and then I sprint out
to truss you in an act of drama, while you
can't move, under neighbouring surveillance.
Then I release you, and you ascend the uneven
steps to find yourself tiny at the top, where
crowds are sparser. In the ancient sound system
copy my lines: *My nation-state for a Porsche.*
The acoustics can't be quite that perfect:
you'll notice the speakers all around us.

*

We waited at Delphi
where the forum foretells

the priests' new brand
is now oracle spam.

Three Euros an hour.
Answers are power.

Where is the centre?
*That way*, they said.

What's chipped on the rock?
*That's the visitor's book.*

These barbarian troops?
*Europe's lost tour groups.*

Is this the crisis?
*Too risky to decide.*

Will the taxi drivers prevail?
*Their calls will be taken.*

Do we have enough water?
*You will not go short.*

Can we escape history?
*In the chariot's dust.*

What will our future be?
Your *future's* a museum.

How long have I got left?
*Check in your letters.*

What is the sense
of a rhetorical question?

Will we make it home safe?
*Your ferry will sail.*

\*


*Hero cult.*
*A beheaded lion.*
*Somebody's rubbish.*

*Carbonized cereal.*
*Rocks on hills.*
*The burnt citadel.*

*A storeroom sacked.*
*Spiral decoration.*
*Underground aqueduct.*

*The silent museum.*
*A replica shop.*
*Echo in the beehive tomb.*

*Unlit cistern.*
*Grasshopper hiding as a leaf.*
*Throne figurine.*

*An anthropomorphic vase.*
*Lizard too quick for the camera.*
Some kennings for the concept of the past

in Linear C, deciphered
on the basis of finds in Mycenae
in the era of crisis.

### brilliant mistake missing me

>

> pale yellow glass bottles curl into Florence Lapis
> curl again into a fluid swan's neck
> to gravity's muffled slant of foreshore
>

> our breath tassels in shells to my ears
> enlightening the equation of compass ends
> physics' might in poiesis
>

> how we grow into an irrational number
> loll of diamond saline from the tongue-curve
> splintering smaller drops before zillions of grains
>

> a permanent non-repeating pattern
> of human phosphorescence
> against you, the sand, and a higher sun
>

> I stand air-lifted into full-auditory clarity
> for a conveyor belt throw of another curl
> and rip of your tongue laughing at me
>

> how easy I am here
> mapped by a parasol-roof
> surf breathing gaps between us
>

> to the ground's ears deepening
> until that momentary flight—
> washes the world out

## aye to see

>

> We may call it herb of grace o' Sundays. They enjoy their own company except on Sunday, the herb's day, when the residents gather in each other's rue gardens to ruminate and play cards from a deck only of clubs; the rue's fleshy oblong leaves. Afterwards, they make their way home in the herbaceous fragrance of rue.

>

> Rue de Rue, is a narrow cobbled-lane where one's soft worn boots can forsake an ankle angled between the mounds. O, you must wear your rue with a difference! Not rueful for such an ankle, the pebbles, lifted from their stream-beds, long for the ocean.

>

> There's rue for you, and here's some for me. The rue not only wards off demons, spells, and spirits, but also those not from the Rue. The Rue de Rue residents spend the rest of the week in their gardens, clipping the perennial rue, indelible to their existence, for no one of this cobble-way wants to leave, aside from the cobblestones knowing the distant roll of ocean. Soles, wheels, and hooves see only their own chipped polishing of the pebbles. Many overlook the cobblestones' lifespan and think Rue de Rue's history short compared to the rue.

>

> The gardeners, that is, the residents of Rue de Rue, trust in the healing powers of the rue. Similarly, the Roman artisans taught the residents how eating the herb improves their eyesight, thus the Rue residents (who keep to themselves) spy the weasels whom they allow to eat the herb, for it gives the weasel strength to fight the snake and rat. King Mithridates VI of Pontus used the rue to guard himself from foes' poison and Hippocrates saw it to relieve rheumatic pains and heart palpitations.

>

> From Ophelia's house her reed tune tolls as she garlands her shrub in speech. And Richard second guesses where his queen weeps in her garden. His remembrance sets a bank of rue.

>

> All are in awe of the rue forever returning, the medicinal shrub seeming to bleed its last vestige to know its gardener, who knows of seasons. So it goes on, forever distracted in rue, even the cobblestones rueful for the sea.

# SIMON SMITH

## Round the Corner

&—back
to Ramsgate this place


of exile—cut
to the edge of my nose
invisible hair's breadth


exposed this morning – turned to
cold – open – air


walking


from street to town & coast the march downhill only Time blocks
    the way &


UKIP's phony nationalism—the junk shop politics of the made-up
    English
the ghost-faced-desperate peddling to the abject—lost


tatty fly-blown out-the-back-
of-a-lock-up – the junk – assume
their position in the price structure of macro-economics


broken down child's pram—a sun-faded pink—
old school chair
purple balloons

& back
tuned to all your ugly arguments


the wall is thin
thinner than the paper flier


'this street's nice except those in that big house across the road'
the Poles are there & handy


once home & turned to *Mmm… Ah Yes* for company
flopped across the Lloyd Loom chair
one leg dangles


## Studio Poem

when consuming a dish of smoked oysters or fois gras
you cannot cannot assume the moral high ground

when looking upon a harbour scene at Cannes
etched on a Hugh Casson plate you cannot

when two generous glasses of Arc du Rhône leave me
purple lipped & purple tongued
there can be no explication—digression only

I was lying half-awake listening for
'Four Dialogues for Two Pianos & Two Voices' & hearing
'is she well or is she ill'—a divided Self—out of sorts

when you fire-bombed my heart—waved & was gone
there are some things to work out with you across a lifetime
so I'm writing you this love note before its too late

like it almost was for the bronze Venus tossed to the heap

I spelt out the word—your word – 'f-e-l-i-c-i-t-y'
which brings me luck (or is it happiness) – so I hope

the half-moon of a wine glass stain
luxuriant on cork & oak
me perfidious in red wine

me leaden headed—an old hand—I've found
ready for another time—
hold the glass to my heart & exhale

you moulding the world into the world with strong fingers

or as pages to form a world bruised & creased—as you see it—
the dark horizon edge below sky
blue sky

or on another day entirely an inevitable sulphurous fog rolls shoreward
The Channel grey & a sickly changeable yellow
that time steering north just around the promenade

or when I brought home to you a crumpled heart
the shape of a valentine—sickly sticky & spat out
your grin flashed bright—keen as a lemon slice

out of an afternoon transformed daylight
the evening sun drifts off into this quarter
of the kitchen glazing the window misted off-white

## Poem

The Queen's Head Acton Road 2013—there you are John James
in a trench coat sat on a stool at the bar sipping rosé


1993—or was it four—the Three Cups Sandland Street John James
clad in black leather jacket leans into the bar buys me a pint of IPA


or was it 1991 at the first CCCP—John strolls about
the stage—flapping leather greatcoat to read 'February'—


    'Schubert spoke to me in the bath
    it came through a hole in the wall the light
    shone through the trees
    & took away our grief
    in saecula saeculorum amen'


strides off to thunderous applause

knocking around a glass
sound of the future rushes away

## Yo

I am so demanding
I expect the humming-

bird to appear
at the anointed hour!

And you pioneer
birch, you there

with your carpet
of leaves the forest resents—

I salute you
I no swinger

of birches or men…
Paper, yellow, white

what are you
thin and perfect

on the lawn?
The spotted fawn

noses below
your waving leaves

and autumn
is welcome

so folded
into a summer so long

we cannot imagine
your limbs bare.

Talking to birches
I am an idiot

& I know you get it
reader—no idiolect

this dialect
riddled with defects

time will fix
or forget.  Whatevs.

It is never not time
to say hello
or goodbye.


## Coyotes

OK you heard the coyotes
and I didn't.

It is always this—
you this, I that

and a canyon
opening between.

Five short yips
and then the known long howl.

You can hear
the highway even here.

# Ralph Hawkins

## By Camel Thorn

see horses in words, the bees in combs and arches in
imagine a world without
a cold plum in space (two pimples, a gastric band, a shower curtain)
viaducts across a ruined cosmic empire
all these "things" we talk of and discuss heartfelt
everything we seemingly need (sweet peas and gnomes)
resistance and consent of ethical demands

---

popped off a few names on my *hit list*
by the camel thorn and chinaberry and the fake alarm clock
I do keep taking the pills
one for a cuckoo twitch—a capsule—where once there was a life
of the mind (which one) with its built in self torture
woodworm, spigots, giant caterpillars

What is the goal of psychoanalysis? (quote)

There, up in the mountains, in the snow leading an authentic life
all of us in our place

drowsy on wormwood

one for asleep and one for a wake

and one for a shopping list

---

*Linne de Passe* 2:30 of an afternoon count your blessings
I'm covered in Dove
ready to sink into my medication, a few chants and ring tones
as white as snow and as Fifi as clouds my memory is unsettled
was it you only a minute ago
whose sails are now on the decrease
dead calm, autochthonic, bill and cooing
ave maria with a little dribble
o madre o madre on a controlled diet

———————————


tenderly with a kiss at the end (it's an x) of a letter (Mr to Mrs Adams?)
what we have here is an asymmetric cheese
an old (x) asteroid sucked in by gravity
bed linen on the line, you grow older by the split second
see the wind in the wind-sock, a pair of tights, a ladder, a goose fair
lots of loose-leaf fluttering of memoria, a blow of sorts,
a lot of waving before the compressional collapse
who fathered these goats who tethered their wills
off in the wind of design (no pun)

## *from* After Swann

52

that trembling condition
not cheerful
not at all unattractive

the cornfields
those little houses
the water's edge

should be
rather like being astonished
so insignificant a creature

a street
outlined upon her lips
an air of hesitation

declared her natural
subjective state

even the sound of this place
aware of her existence

a series of high notes approaching
sudden reflection

peculiar, volatile pleading—
the torrents of rain

its uniform meshes
like a cloudy halo
possessing her wholly

53

she had been obliged
that custom
daily

a distaste
she wrote
on paper

the gas-jets
gone
motionless, before

that other self
the petals
and the 'letter-heading'

full of love
which modifies the fullness
the illusion

that one is listening
in a stoup of
the air

pure and
invisible
a world of ultra-violet

the momentary
crowd
disguised

in sound
every word
in exile and alone

the vanity of
his love

a digression

it had codified
*motifs*
of another order


54

veiled in
the little phrase
five notes

of a frigid
contracted sweetness
compose

the emotion
a clouded surface
of sound

of bodily desire
vanished
something less bitter

so loving, so
blunting itself
some admirable

syllogism
Audacity
charming the dialogue

like a bird
somewhere lamenting
splendour

hierophants
incapable of perceiving
her first assertion

## A Listening Station

you now enter
the not-for-profit sector
cannot contain good news
for the Turks and North Africa
compete to sell me
'the Red Army' hats & signs
hot dog stands by
Chinese restaurant or
occupies part of the site
intended to inspire awe once
for a millennium
pieces that vain
date debris
building project
unearthed by workers
digging to replace Soviet block
for housing component of the privileged
with shiny office
of multinational banks

memorial to fallen leaves or
jump & swing among teenagers and
mothers with strollers converse
the phones lit
with elegantly suited apparatchiks
enterprise museum
souvenir stand
multimedia presentation (with
interactive touchscreen symbolism
added & fries) or
US corporation that flag
flies through it all
illuminated by reflected glow of the spotlight
gracefully from the setting sun

the heart is a mountain road
in east-west direction running
unfinished and already secured
with a fence
the devil hills'
walls equipped with ears

the ministry did not confirm or deny
or she holds any information within
mountain gravel cover
the unfinished building of the university
of a defence that has nothing but a number
but some demolition was
already some foundations & pattern
from the attic to the end of work

amorphous materials from room 75/038
a mass of paper yarn and black fleck
telephone conversation among the party elite
comprehension of high priority
a motor mechanic with a list of employees & why
they might be enticed insight
into weakness exploited

immured incinerator liftshaft & shredders self-
domestic facilities for staff
including wood-panelled courtyard lined
intelligence personnel and linguists
drill a hole in the floor a dark interior
all samples a high fibre count
structural black fleck could be remnants
of carbon paper: where do these
documents now? high
mineral content of the material &
frequency of entomological
violation of the site reflect low pollen
and plant material evidence
the lack of windows

on each bus or U-Bahn
women hold property eye
in context of busy crowded
hustle & bustle & jostle it
on the tray of cake
in plastic fragile shell

the night S-Bahn
man is too fat to be contained
in one place part one of the thighs & seat
& unleashed trainer/coach rendering the
opposite unoccupiable
lolls snoring ears plugged
with Sony products
& probably misses his stop

excavators were far below
fugitives who crave jeans & Marlboro
those obedient staff
mining data
whose whereabouts & progress
day-by-day calm loyalty
& possible death have been reported
for those whose movements are directed
secretly intercept
because a man which Blake by name
incorrectly credited ideology
is pressured into private life
or enjoys to play spy

in river while digging piles
for the new
construction & excavator grab
every silver object of devotion & ritual
cast on the waters
by the 'minions of history'
battered & blackened on
night of pogrom and infamous

for those few recusants
who else might put faith
in doctrines gone to the wall
should be a daily bile flavour
in advertising at bus stops wrily
Toys R Us for the Karl-Marx-Straße

## PErIoDyC AuPoCAlYPSe
How the world was (un)made in 7 days


Day 1


FYRe, EuArTh, TiN, WAtEr, PINe.


Day 2


GeNTlYbURn TaCTiCl ThORaXeS, CuPtHe HoTmAmArY In LiFe.
MoBrGaAsSm... PuPa Cd SiTcAgGd, BiNd FIr-LaCe,
FrOsTbITe, BaRe CoNe, MnK ScAt SeWNiNa H(fErN)p


Day 3


CoMnInGeLa HeAt SeAm W BeAr FeCeS, TaAsTe RaPtURe
ClOsEuP. SiTiNa CaSm - CLiF 'Nd CrAg, RuBi HoTlOv.
NeIThEr Cd Cm BaAcK.


Day 4


BaYbAlNz: HeRbHoDy — AmOsSey CAsTl, AgRaNd RuIn,
MoISTe LiPoNa BeAcH BLuF.

                    FeAr AtTaKXe!

SiNbIrDs FlUutRh Uup, BrInGeNTiRe ClOTh. CoVEr
PUBiCfLaW.


Day 5
PoPE's PuNiScHMt, NaSTi. FLaY BAcKSrAuW, CUut LuV
FrMoUuoRh HoLi HeArTe. FlInGa FeTl CuRuSe On Al
EuTaErI

## Day 6

SPaN FeNzEs AcRhOs BaRe PLaNeTc, HeM'g In BeAuTiUus
FlUXe. BiND CaScH VAlLu LiK MoBhErDs CuUut-Uup Fr
CUuoPoNbBk.

(M)tArSnDy GaRbAg BAtHs, CoRuPt As TaZrSiNa ClAmY
PuL(v)Se - thEuIr HoTeMnBr OF RaGe NoW ICe.

## Day 7

BhUup FlUusHsEs, NoDs UuoUut.

Notes:

There are currently 118 known elements on this planet. The first 98, up
through Californium (Cf), are naturally occurring. The final 20 exist
only when synthetically created. "PErIODyC AuPoCAlYPSe" recounts
civilization's rise and incursion into nature, as told by the 118 elements
themselves (for what else do we really have?). The first three days are
constructed solely from natural elements. Synthetic elements begin to
creep in at the end of day four, where they continue their ascent for two
more days until all natural elements have been consumed or extirpated,
leaving only synthetic elements to conclude the tale on the final day.

# ELŻBIETA WÓJCIK-LEESE

## Nordhavn Offerings

'In this way, when I write bougie and so evoke light, on the inside the Italian word bugia, which means lie, is "lunging" and attracting around it a darker semantic field.'

(Jean Portante)


4 MAY 2011
today only the spilt glare
                    signals the sea        *havet : morze*


5 MAY 2011
the horizontals care
               fully displayed
against the turbines and cranes      *turbiny*


7 MAY 2011
the blue underlined
    with emerald
        or is it turquoise      *turkus*


8 MAY 2011
lustre of the littoral
               underpaths    *of Polish*

^^^

the white spotting of a whale
         ferry—breathturning    *my first language lunging*

9 MAY 2011
the right half of the harbour
outsparkles the left                    *left for languages*


10 MAY 2011
two bulging lamps slowly slide back
        as the ship pushes forward    *Danish wedges itself*
                                       *between Polish and English*

11 MAY 2011
a sudden raft topped with
                              orange
        sits squarely midwater         *svimmelt hen over det hvide*


12 MAY 2011
mute wind turbines mill the
        haze on the horizon           *pijane ponad bielą*


15 MAY 2011
one turbine has stopped
                mesmerized
by the slate hulk tearing itself
                off the coast          *dizzy over the white*


19 MAY 2011
the punch card of portholes
slotted into
the row of S-tog windows              *Ord som flade fisk der flaprede*


23 MAY 2011
the golden streak clearly claims
                larger
                much larger area       *Words like flat fish that flapped*

24 MAY 2011
smeared in the rain drops
extinguished by the grey
electricity shack                    *Bathing in a drop's quiet light*


25 MAY 2011
early morning, concealed by the red of the S-train
early afternoon, the red revealed in the rescue
          boat on the pewter waves    *Bader mig i en dråbes stille lys*


30 MAY 2011
                    shimmering flatness
waves resting to ripples Monday—
tired with
              their routine        *mig (my) submerged in English*


31 MAY 2011
one wind turbine scooping the warm
                              sheen
in the corner of
the train window            *me : mig : mnie emerging to breathe*


NOTES:
*svimmelt.../ Ord.../ Bader ...* —Pia Tafdrup, 'Min Mors Hånd,'
      *Dronningeporten* (Gyldendal, 1998)
*dizzy.../ Words.../ Bathing...* —David McDuff's translation of
      Tafdrup: 'My Mother's Hand,' *Queen's Gate* (Bloodaxe, 2001)
*pijane...* —my translation of Tafdrup's Danish and McDuff's English
      into Polish (Copenhagen, 2011)

## *from* Thixotropic Tarot

you have to start
somewhere

0. The Fool
[press 'enter']

**YC.1993.a.1574**
tiresias is / time
for tea cupped in hir
hands: change

1.

Designer pineapple realigns into explosive molecules:
"I could not experiment on this phenomenon
often enough":

zhe reads
(W. Mulford):

*haunting the voice line*

*drafted to oracle by*
~~[redacted]~~

tiresias speaks only in shibboleths
hir words a 'stream, torrent' ghosted

in the machine
but not of it
*contemporary*
*drowning*

form and phenomenon collapse into tautology.

1. The Magician
[next slide, please]

97

I aim to learn genetic programming in order
to tackle these design problems.


the experiment
(by Bruno Munari):

*an iron sculpture*

*destroyed*

*then*
*reduced to dust &*
*sprinkled evenly*
*over an aluminum surface*
*under which magnets are*

*agitated*

One works to make
oneself obsolete:
"Animus qui hoc
involavit et qui
conscious fuerit
ut
eum decipias
defixio"

                            use sparingly

1.5

    Macaronics & ligatures:

the machine-speak of
    reality. One stitch in time saves
                      nine.

                Pull one loop through all these other
                                      loops.
                    (Only one stitch active.)

A crotchety Tiresias enters the godhead:

>                   2: The High Priestess
>                    [will see you now]
> the primitive form of my resistance
> forms a node—
>         resistors function as a branching point.

2.

A virtual topology:
the rain stutters densely.
A mantra of destroyed directed paths
beneath
a chorus making the plea for recombination.

>                 *strange to have a storm at this time of year*
>                 *lightning thunder i am trying to remember*
>                 *when there was no punishment. i shall not*
>                 *criticize. we must suffer. it is hard.*

>                 strange: tiresias is rose-
>                 gazing with grace lake / ripples
>                 reflect the ripped sky on her surface

>                               and beneath
>                              they are holding
>                            (such things as) hands
>                                   open
>                                  enter /
>                                  / safe //
>                               combination

On this summer's day
the sky unlocks
and a lone starling
missing one eye
falls to the ground.

tiresias

3: The Empress

[a.k.a. electronic tether]

mood/ring/torque/crown

discovers the missing cog

continues

3.

~~endures~~ no ~~survives~~
~~no~~ continues no
hir "no" is hir
continuum

tiresias realising the phenomenon of rippling

in pieces

is forced to study the coagulation process.

Tiresias' translation app is unreliable: Babel
(fish-food) goddedegook
asset-stripping
idiolects, platelets
(declination)

4. The Emperor

[YouTube to the nation]

We are no longer bodies.

We are what it means to

have a body.

We are soon to be stories

our insides marked by irreversible periodicity.

4.

An unsolved equation:
Alice becoming larger and smaller simultaneously.

*The child in the snow has found her mouth.*
The child has found snow in her mouth.
The child in her mouth has found snow.
The snow-in-mouth has found her child.

tiresias, tired, reads
Veronica Forrest-Thomson's line as risk

all fall
all fall
wall & wall & wall

tiresias crochets his fingers
becomes bivocal:

an echo
of a planet-spanning gene pool

5: The Hierophant
<stet>
of sensations

5.

Wet glass: these extra layers
are not accessible
from the outside.

tiresias is hir own google
searches °°condensation°°

We simulate learning
through format restoration.
A parlando of extracted protoypes
might provide the appropriate response:

"condensation reaction
condensation definition
condensation polymerisation
condensation synthesis
condensation nuclei
condensation pump"

tiresias is thinking up ways of crossing

All italicised quotations from Denise Riley, ed. *Poets on Writing* (Basingstoke:
Macmillan, 1992)

# PETER HUGHES

## Five Petrarch Sonnets

### 1 / 128

*O passi sparsi, o pensier' vaghi et pronti*

I wandered bony as a cod thrown back
on misplaced oceanic tendencies
several loads of wool arrive from England
as I wiggle my way up the Arno

towards another afternoon of Glück
I should send her one of those messages
that never arrive—or arrive too late
or precipitate the final crisis

amongst all the posing & corruption
three pigeons are eating one cornetto
with what looks a lot like civility

I write down eternity addressed to
my Madonna of the Pomegranate
although she hates it when I call her that


### 2 / 129

*Lieti fiori et felici, et ben nate herbe*

I'm permitted to return to meadows
which are memories of words she never said
where sunlight I imagined is pouring
down through dancing gaps in her foliage

each thought of her turns into two or three
more & more going up in a spiral
sprouting perky tufts of these angelic
notions floating away towards the sea

we are further than ever from knowing
what a thought such as natural could mean
she shifts the constitution of each scene

many nooks & fringes of the landscape
have been radically singed & strangely
furred by exposure to my thermal vents


## 3 / 130

*Amor, che vedi ogni pensero aperto*

when love & I agree to take a hike
we pretend it's scheduled preparation
for some overwhelming challenge such as
bush-tucker trials of the late Renaissance

even though we're never going to make it
& introducing contemporaries
into religious or performance art
gets easier after Masaccio

in the distance a certain radiance
may modify the flavour of despair
but the glowing promise of fulfilment

has a tendency to end up nothing
but a radioactive effusion
compromising everybody's prospects

## *from* Stigmata

I hear that you're adding up
my years in work for my old age pension:
1 year a labourer for a drainage company,
2 years a soldier with former convicts,
3 years an accountant in the farming industry,
3 years a labourer & field guard in a tomato farm,
9 months a book warehouse man,
2 years a Lang & Lit teacher in a high school,
7 years a hand labourer in the Ciociaria,
2 years on the black market,
3 years with stamps
& the rest back on the black market.
Amen.

\*


In black I've also written my songs
for the white people of the solar continent,
who know me by fame & not by the famine
that hollows my self like shadow does a valley stream.
If I exist, it's only through your voice,
if I die, only in your thirst,
if I'm reborn, only from your mud.
Over me the loud walls of your memories crumble
& the tender space of grass meadows closes in.
How hard it is to live at the border of one voice, your voice,
even knowing that salvation moves through the light of names
& the mortal dust of the arenas.
For years I've failed to understand what happens inside me,
surrounded by the knowing skin of the blind
& by the deaf words of those who leave at daybreak
without looking back.

\*

I write day & night.

Rivers of black verse,
pages & pages filling
without respite.

My books like the villages
bomb-blitzed at sundown,
my verses like rows of mournful monks
praying for me.

*

I'm not stealing either your riches or your glory,
I don't aim to possess anything but my own body,
it is written even in the dusts that I've come from
and in the memory of the trees
clustered tight all around me.

My roads do not return to water,
my room catches on fire every night.

Years spent in wait & I'm waiting for no one
to come to my house.

My soul a shattered mirror,
a bird fallen in the rain
with the blind who won't stop looking for light
in the night's darkness.

I am looking for new paths on which to flee
carrying my bloodied secret.

*

It's my skin rings out, slung on the sunset,
heralding bloodied bulls in summer's fields,
fireflies around the valleys,
lyrical bird flights along the river banks.

It's my skin calls out, slung on the sunset,
it calls out so when springtime comes,
dreaming of poppies and pathways.

It's my skin listens out, slung on the sunset,
searching for my Voice through the fog
of another alphabet.

*


With my nights born of your days
I will reach as far as your dry lips,
I, the survivor of dictatorships
that obliterate every freedom
will knock as if at the door of a holy city,
forbidden to infidels.

*


My body's shaking,
my blood is dancing,
my veins are singing,
I'm no longer me.
Bit by bit I burn
like wax in a hastily abandoned temple,
little by little I lose my way
in the chasm of Time.
In my hands I have the nests of bee-eaters,
in my eyes I have your snows.
If you see deserts, they grow on my skin,
if you see lightning, it enters my flesh,
if you see murderers, they dwell around my heart.
I've never been this amazed at myself,
I walk among passers-by & shout out loud:
"O people I accept the judgement
& won't break out of my own mud."

# NOTES ON CONTRIBUTORS

THEODOROS CHIOTIS studied Classics and Modern Languages at the universities of London and Oxford. His work in English has appeared, in *Adventures in Form* (Penned in the Margins), *Otoliths, Catechism: Poems for Pussy Riot* (English Pen), *Tears in the Fence, Fit to Work: Poets Against ATOS* and *Bad Robot Poetry.*

PATRICIA DEBNEY's second collection, *Littoral,* was published by Shearsman in 2013. She teaches at the University of Kent.

CARRIE ETTER has published two collections, one each with Seren and Shearsman; Seren will publish her third in 2014. Shearsman published her anthology of women's experimental poetry, *Infinite Difference,* in 2010.

CHARLOTTE FABER lives in London. *Salt* is her first complete collection of poetry.

KIM GOLDBERG is a winner of the Rannu Fund Poetry Prize for Speculative Literature and a finalist for Canada's Gerald Lampert Award for *Ride Backwards on Dragon,* her lyrical journey through ancient martial arts and Taoist alchemy. She holds a degree in Biology and is an avid birdwatcher and nature lover on Vancouver Island. Visit her online at www.PigSquashPress.com.

GËZIM HAJDARI was born in 1957 in Hajdaraj, Albania. Because of his outspoken opposition to the régime and the post-Communist government, he was forced to leave Albania in 1992 following repeated threats. Since 1993 Hajdari, who writes both in Albanian and Italian, has published twelve collections of poetry, two travel books, and a long essay (*Albanian Epicedium*) in memory of the poets and writers imprisoned and murdered under Hoxha. His poetry has been translated into several languages and has won many awards. He has lived in exile in Frosinone, Italy, since 1992.

GRAHAM HARDIE's poetry has been published in a number of magazines. His latest collection can be bought at http://www.efpress.com/tsoa.htm. He is 41, lives just outside Glasgow and works as a gardener.

MICHAEL HASLAM's collected earlier poems are available from Shearsman as *Mid-Life* (2007); subsequent writings, collected in three volumes as the *Music* series are published by Arc. *A Cure for Woodness* (2010) is the most recent.

RALPH HAWKINS has published many collections, two of them with Shearsman: *The MOON, the Chief Hairdresser (Highlights)* (2004) and *Goodbye to Marzipan* (2009).

JEREMY HOOKER's collected poems, *The Cut of the Light* was published by Enitharmon in 2006. Shearsman published his *Upstate — A North American Journal* in 2007 and will publish his *Openings — A European Journal* next year.

ALEX HOUEN is co-editor of *Blackbox Manifold*. His poetry has appeared in a variety of magazines, and he is author of *Powers of Possibility: Experimental American Writing since the 1960s* (Oxford UP, 2012). He teaches at the University of Cambridge.

PETER HUGHES runs Oystercatcher Press in Norfolk. He has three Shearsman collections, including a *Selected Poems* (2013). Shearsman also published a book of essays on his work, edited by Ian Brinton, under the title, *'An intuition of the particular'* (2013).

JOHN JAMES lives in Cambridge and in Puisserguier in the Languedoc. His most recent books include *In Romsey Town* (Equipage, 2011) and *Cloud Breaking Sun* (Oystercatcher Press, 2012). A *Collected Poems* appeared from Salt in 2002.

MARIA JASTRZĘBSKA was born in Warsaw, came to England as a child, and now lives in Brighton. Her third full-length collection *At The Library of Memories* was published by Waterloo Press, 2013. Her drama *Dementia Diaries* toured nationally in 2011.

KELLY MALONE lives in Auckland, NZ. She is currently working on her first full collection of poetry. She has previously published in *Turbine, Potroast, NZEPC, SWAMP,* and *Brief.* She has a Masters of Creative Writing and a Masters of Arts from the University of Auckland.

SOPHIE MAYER is a poet and activist, co-editing *Binders Full of Women, Fit to Work: Poets against Atos* and *Solidarity Park Poetry.* She has published two full collections: *Her Various Scalpels* (Shearsman) and *The Private Parts of Girls* (Salt), and two chapbooks: *Kiss Off* (Oystercatcher) and, with Sarah Crewe, *signs of the sistership* (Knives, Forks and Spoons).

MARION MCCREADY lives on the west coast of Scotland. Her poems have appeared in a variety of journals and magazines. Her poetry pamphlet collection, *Vintage Sea,* was published by Calder Wood Press (2011).

MAUREEN N. MCLANE is the author of three books of poems, including the forthcoming *This Blue* (Farrar Straus and Giroux, 2014); she also recently published a book of experimental prose, *My Poets* (FSG, 2012), a hybrid of memoir and criticism.

GEORGE MESSO has three collections from Shearsman, most recently *Violades & Appledown* (2012), and is a widely-published translator from Turkish. His anthology *Ikinci Yeni* was shortlisted for the Popescu Prize.

ALISTAIR NOON's publications include *Earth Records* (Nine Arches Press, 2012); translations include Pushkin's *The Bronze Horseman* (Longbarrow) and Monika Rinck's *16 Poems* (Barque). He lives in Berlin.

KAT PEDDIE is a PhD student and assistant lecturer at the University of Kent. She works on modern American poetry. She is the co-editor of the poetry magazine *Zone.* Her poems have also appeared in *Tears in the Fence.*

MARTHE REED is the author of three books, most recently *(em)bodied bliss* (Moria Books 2013). A fourth book, *Pleth*, is in press and a fifth will be published in 2014. She has also published four chapbooks as part of the Dusie Kollektiv.

DENISE RILEY lives in London. Her many books include *'Am I that Name?'* *Feminism and the Category of Women in History* (1988) and *Impersonal Passion: Language As Affect* (2005). She edited *Poets on Writing; Britain 1970-1991* (1992) and her own poetry includes *Penguin Modern Poets 10* with Oliver and Sinclair (1996) and *Denise Riley: Selected Poems* (2000).

ANTONY ROWLAND has published two collections, *The Land of Green Ginger* (Salt, 2008) and *I Am a Magenta Stick* (Salt, 2012). He has awarded the Manchester Poetry Prize in 2012. His work has been anthologised in *Identity Parade: New British and Irish Poets* (Bloodaxe, 2010).

AIDAN SEMMENS lives in Suffolk. His first collection, *A Stone Dog* (2011) was published by Shearsman, as was his Suffolk anthology, *By the North Sea* (2013). Parlor Press published *The Book of Isaac* in the USA in 2012.

LUCY SHEERMAN lives in Cambridge. Oystercatcher Press published *rarefied: falling without landing* in 2012. She was recently commissioned by Menagerie to write a short play *What did it feel like to go to the Moon?* based on a collaboration with the Apollo 15 astronaut and poet Al Worden.

SIMON SMITH has published three books with Salt, the latest being *London Bridge*. He has also published a pamphlet, *Gravesend*, with Veer Books in 2011. Shearsman will publish his collection, *11781 W. Sunset Boulevard*, in 2014. His translations from Catullus will appear shortly from Carcanet.

DONNA STONECIPHER's publications include three poetry volumes, most recently *The Cosmopolitan* (Coffee House Press, 2008). Her translations include Ludwig Hohl: *Ascent* (Black Square Editions). She lives in Berlin.

NATHAN THOMPSON has two Shearsman collections, *the arboretum towards the beginning* (2008) and *The Visitor's Guest* (2011).

CRISTINA VITI is a widely-published poet and translator. Her translation of Mariapia Veladiano's award-winning novel *A Life Apart* was published by MacLehose Press in Spring 2013, and a new version of Dino Campana's *Orphic Songs* is forthcoming from Waterloo Press.

JOHN WELCH has a long publishing history. From Shearsman: a memoir, *Dreaming Arrival* and *Collected Poems* (both 2008), *Visiting Exile* (2009) and *Its Halting Measure* (2012).

ELŻBIETA WÓJCIK-LEESE is a writer and a translator of contemporary Polish poetry. Her recent publications include: *Nothing More* (translations from Krystyna Miłobędzka, Arc 2013); *Metropoetica* (co-written with 'women writing cities', Seren 2013).